Level Up Gaming

LEVEL UP MINECRAFT

LORI DITTMER

BLACK RABBIT BOOKS

Bolt is published by Black Rabbit Books
P.O. Box 227, Mankato, Minnesota, 56002.
www.blackrabbitbooks.com

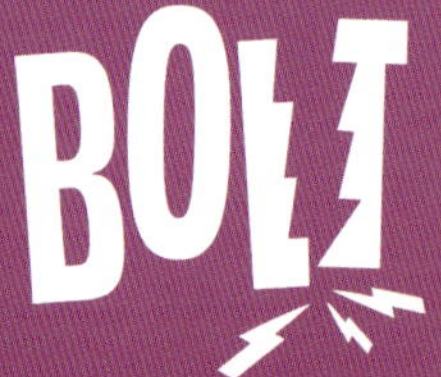

Alissa Thielges, editor; Rhea Magaro, designer and photo researcher

Library of Congress Cataloging-in-Publication Data
Names: Dittmer, Lori author
Title: Level up Minecraft / Lori Dittmer.
Description: Mankato, MN: Black Rabbit Books, [2026] | Series: Level up gaming | Includes bibliographical references and index. | Audience: Ages 8-12 | Audience: Grades 4-6
Identifiers: LCCN 2025017483 (print) | LCCN 2025017484 (ebook) | ISBN 9781645824794 library binding | ISBN 9781645824879 ebook
Subjects: LCSH: Minecraft (Game)—Juvenile literature
Classification: LCC GV1469.35.M535 D58 2026 (print) | LCC GV1469.35.M535 (ebook) | DDC 794.8—dc23/eng/20250621
LC record available at https://lccn.loc.gov/2025017483
LC ebook record available at https://lccn.loc.gov/2025017484

Printed in China

Image Credits

Dreamstime/Aleksandr Dorogin, 32, Roberto Bellomonte, 17; Mojang Studios, 6, 7, 8, 9, 11, 12, 14, 15, 16, 19, 21, 22–23, 28, 31; Pastelrepair, 4–5; patrika, 20; Shutterstock/AI Generator, cover, 1, 16, aslysun, 27, GizemG, 24–25, klyaksun, 26, lera lysenko, 25, mkfilm, 3.

Every effort has been made to contact copyright holders for material reproduced in this book. Any omissions will be rectified in subsequent printings if notice is given to the publisher.

CONTENTS

CHAPTER 1

Zombie Attack!

Steve digs in a cave. He gathers some iron. He hears a noise. A zombie is at the mouth of the cave. Oh no! It's going to attack! Steve's wolf fights back. The zombie loses! Steve rides a horse to get back home before dark. He is safe from other monsters.

Choose Your Character

Steve

Ari

Sunny

Noor

Alex

Minecraft Beginnings

Minecraft is a sandbox game. Players are free to wander anywhere. There are more than 50 **biomes**. These include swamps, deserts, and forests.

Players can build at their own pace. They can play alone or together. They can also share their world online.

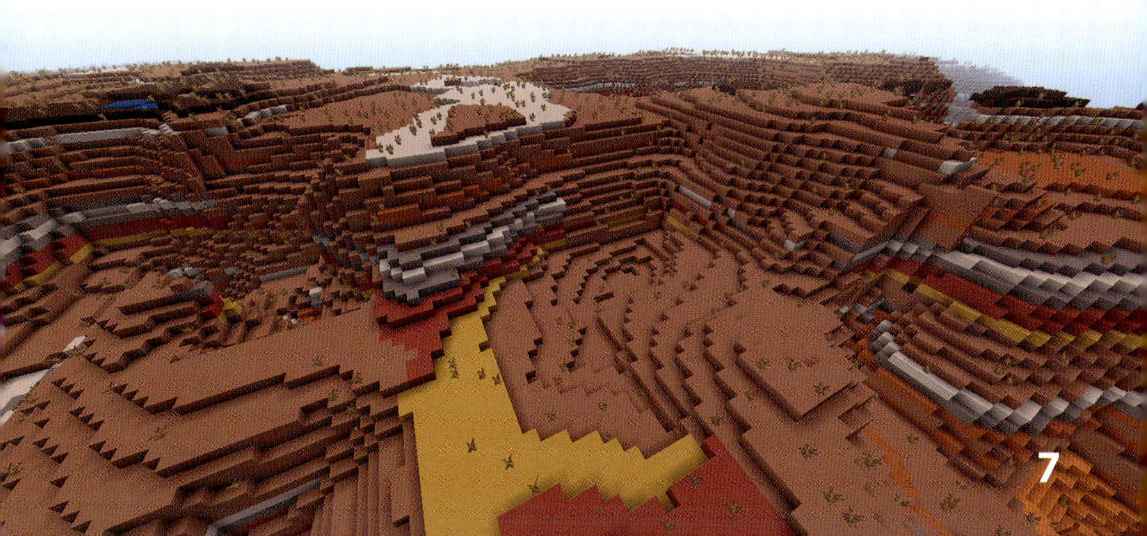

Plain

Flat spaces for building a base.

Forest

Lots of wood for crafting.

Savanna

Find horses and llamas.

Beach

Find food in the ocean.

CHAPTER 2

To begin, the character drops into an open world. Everything is made of blocks. To find **resources**, players break the blocks. Punch a tree to get wood. Then use the wood blocks to make **planks**. Four planks make a crafting table. This table is used to make tools. Tools help farm and mine.

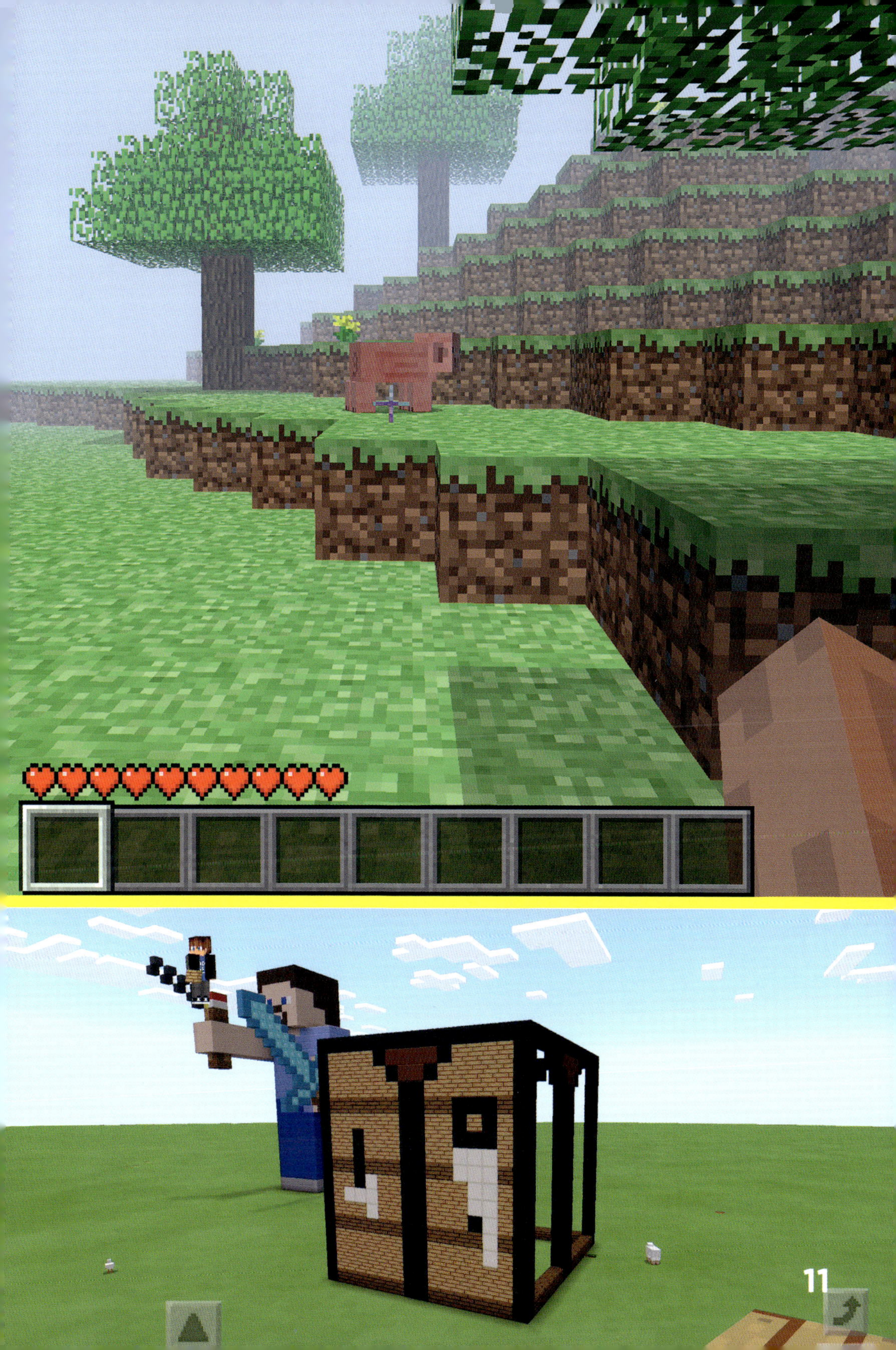

Game Modes

SURVIVAL
survive and build

HARDCORE
only one life

ADVENTURE
player-created world

CREATIVE
unlimited blocks

SPECTATOR
watch a world

A day in *Minecraft* takes 20 minutes.

Minecraft Modes

Players can choose from a few **modes**. The most popular is survival. Players must eat and find resources. They build and craft items. At night, unfriendly **mobs** appear. In creative mode, players build freely. They do not worry about health or hunger. Nothing will attack them.

PASSIVE

Do not attack. They can give friendship and food.

NEUTRAL

May attack if angered. Some give items to players.

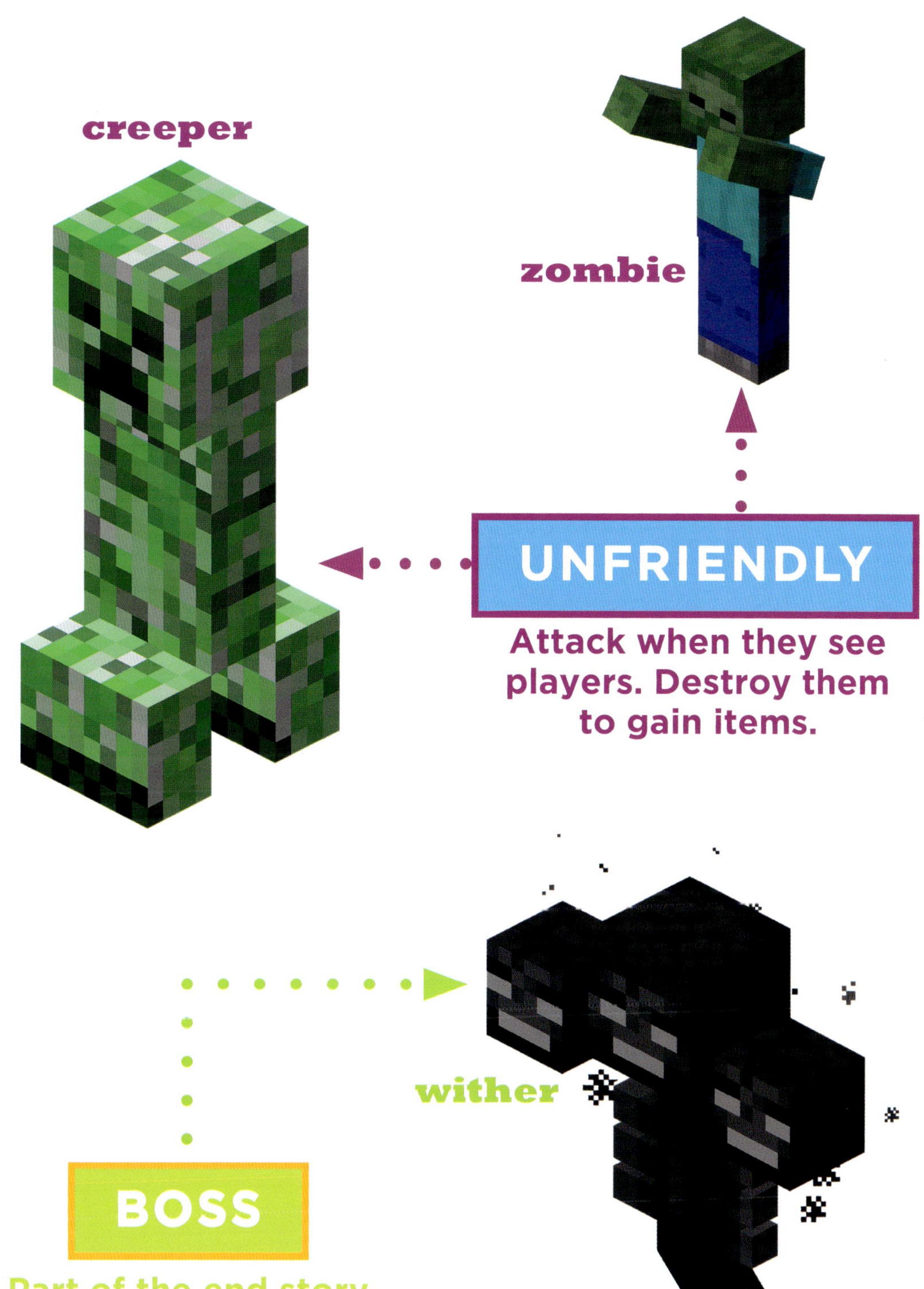
creeper
zombie
UNFRIENDLY
Attack when they see players. Destroy them to gain items.
wither
BOSS
Part of the end story. Destroy them to win.

Build a chest to store items. If your character dies, the tools in the chest will be safe. Otherwise, you might lose them.

Build Your Base

In survival mode, monsters attack. Players need a house to live through the night. Dig into the side of a hill. Or build walls with blocks. Then add a roof. Use torches to keep monsters away. Don't forget a bed! The bed is a **spawn** spot. If your character dies, they will reappear there.

CHAPTER 3

Leveling Up

Mining is the best way to level up. It is one of the most important activities in the game. It helps bring in resources. These are needed for almost everything in *Minecraft*.

First create a stone pickaxe. Then mine for iron. Remember to **upgrade** and create new tools. Better tools dig deeper and faster.

Finding Resources

coal

mountains, caves

caves, deep valleys

deep underground

badlands

Level Up with XP

Players collect experience points (XP). They can use XP to fix and improve tools. There are many ways to get XP. One way is to go fishing. For every item caught, players gain XP. Trading with villagers also gains XP. For a bigger challenge, fight and destroy mobs.

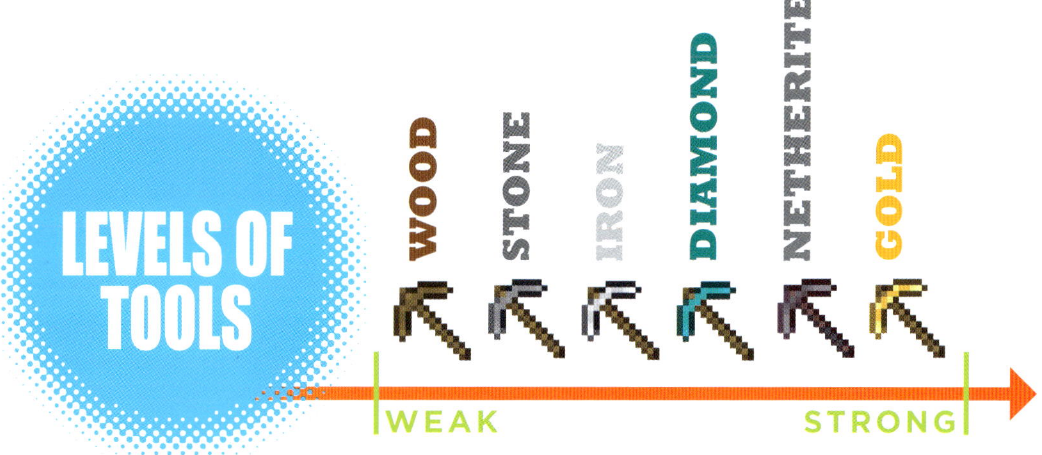

CHAPTER 4

MASTERING MINECRAFT

Creative mode has no end. Players are free to mine and build. Some have built copies of the Titanic and the Taj Mahal. Others made the world from *Lord of the Rings*.

Survival mode has quests. Players pick which ones to complete. The final goal is to beat the Ender Dragon. It can take hundreds of hours of play.

Hardcore mode is part of survival. Only the most skilled play this way!

BUILD THE EARTH
4,000
NUMBER OF BUILDERS.
#1
Biggest *Minecraft* build ever!
CREATOR:
PippenFTS

2020
Year building began. It is still ongoing.
One block =
3.3 feet
(1 meter)

Teaming Up

Minecraft is also an **esport**. Every year, more schools add teams. Teams face off to complete a build. Build battles are timed events. Players are scored on creativity and detail.

Other players **stream** their game online. They share tips. They help people find new ways to beat monsters.

Online Playground

Minecraft is one of the most popular video games of all time. Anyone can play. They can create anything they imagine. Daring players face monsters on quests. They battle a boss to beat the game. Then they play again. They are the masters of their world.

GLOSSARY

biome (BAHY-ohm)—a large, naturally occurring place where specific animals and plants live

esport (EE-spawrt)—competitive video gaming

mob (MOB)—a non-player character that can move around the game world

mode (MOHD)—a set of rules within a game that changes how it is played

plank (PLANGK)—a long, thick board

resource (REE-sohrs)—a concept or element that can be measured or counted and is controlled by the player

spawn (SPAWN)—when a character or object appears in a game, usually in a particular location

stream (STREEM)—to send or receive video or audio material over the internet in a steady flow

upgrade (uhp-GREYD)—to make something better

BOOKS

Downs, Kieran. *Minecraft.* Minneapolis: Bellwether, 2025.

Grack, Rachel. *Curious about Minecraft.* Mankato, MN: Amicus, 2024.

Wagner, Zelda. *Minecraft Creative Mode: Unofficial Gamer Guide.* Minneapolis: Lerner Publications, 2025.

WEBSITES

How to Play Minecraft
www.minecraft.net/en-us/minecraft-tips-for-beginners

Tips and Tricks
www.ign.com/wikis/minecraft/Tips_and_Tricks

Top 10 Facts about Minecraft!
www.funkidslive.com/learn/top-10-facts/top-10-facts-about-minecraft/

INDEX